The Enchanted Horse

Stories from *The Arabian Nights*
Retold by Jamila Gavin
Series Advisor Professor Kimberley Reynolds
Illustrated by Rachel Cloyne

OXFORD
UNIVERSITY PRESS

Letter from the Author

The Arabian Nights was one of
the first fat books of stories on my
bookshelf; stories I have loved ever
since I was a young child. These
tales are so rich and fabulous, that
they have also inspired music, art,
pantomime, ballet and film, and
many of the collections published
throughout hundreds of years have been
illustrated by some of the greatest artists.

There was no one creator of these stories, no one
country from which they came, and no one period in
which they were written. Many were born out of folklore
and seem to be extremely ancient indeed. So they are a
glorious mishmash of cultures: Arabian caliphs, Persian
princes, Bengali princesses, Kashmiri sultans, African
sorcerers and Chinese tailors.

My imagination was fed and watered by these exotic
tales. I hope you will enjoy my retelling of just three
of them – including the introductory story of how
Scheherazade saved herself from death – and that you
will read the rest some day, and be enchanted forever,
as I was.

Jamila Gavin

Long, long ago in ancient times, a most worthy and eminent King of Persia had two sons, Princes Shahriar and Shahzenan. Both of them followed in their father's footsteps and were beloved for their virtue, wisdom and prudence. When, in due course, the old King died, Prince Shahriar mounted the throne but, as he loved and trusted his younger brother, he gave him the kingdom of Samarkand in Great Tartary.

Ten years passed, and the brothers had not seen each other because their kingdoms were so far apart. Desiring to lay eyes once more on his beloved brother, King Shahriar sent his prime minister, the vizier, to Samarkand with a message beseeching Shahzenan to come and visit him.

Shahzenan was deeply moved, and told the vizier that since his kingdom of Tartary was stable and at peace, he could leave for Persia within ten days. So the vizier pitched his tents and waited for the King so that they could travel together.

At last all the preparations had been made. Shahzenan bade a fond farewell to his most beloved

wife and, with his retinue, departed on their long journey. At nightfall, the caravan train set up camp, but after eating and drinking and conversing till nearly midnight, Shahzenan had a sudden yearning to see his wife one last time before such a long separation. So he got on his horse and returned speedily to his palace.

To his shock and inexpressible grief, he came

upon his wife plotting with his enemies to have him overthrown. Before they were even aware of his presence, Shahzenan plunged among them with his flashing scimitar, killing his wife and all the conspirators, and returned to the camp. The next day, without saying a word to anyone, he was ready at dawn to continue the journey towards Persia. But his wife's treachery preyed upon his spirits, and he was seized with great melancholy. Even when they arrived at his brother's kingdom with much beating of kettledrums and joyful music, he could not banish his intense sadness.

King Shahriar embraced him joyfully and, after Shahzenan had bathed and changed his attire, he joined his brother over a celebratory feast. How they talked and laughed and reminisced over old times long into the night and, for a while, Shahzenan forgot about his wife's disloyalty. But once he and his brother had parted for the night, and he had retired to the privacy of his chamber, Shahzenan was again tormented by the treacherous actions of his wife and members of his court.

Unable to sleep, he paced up and down wondering why the people he loved and trusted had turned against him. He examined his own character: perhaps it was his fault; had he been an unjust king, or a bad husband, that his own wife and courtiers were prepared to betray him?

Days went by, and, of course, Shahriar noticed that his brother seemed afflicted by some deep sadness. He tried to divert him with much entertainment of one sort or another, and organized a great two-day hunting match. But Shahzenan excused himself. 'I don't feel too well,' he explained. 'Please forgive me, dear Brother. I'll rest in my chamber. Go and enjoy yourself.' So, reluctantly, Shahriar continued without him.

Alone in his chamber, Shahzenan sat on his balcony overlooking the palace garden, nursing his confusion and bitterness, when suddenly, a secret gate he hadn't noticed before opened, and out came his brother's wife. Believing that she had two whole days to do as she pleased, she now came with an entourage of courtiers, and they gathered

underneath Shahzenan's balcony, thinking he too had gone on the hunt. But sitting quietly above, unseen, he heard every word they said. To his deep dismay, Shahzenan realized that Shahriar's adored wife was plotting to have him overthrown too.

As if the thunder clouds had parted, he looked up to the heavens. Now he understood; now he was sure that it wasn't because he or his brother had done anything wrong, but that it was the nature of women. 'How could I have believed I was the only one to have the misfortune of a treacherous wife?' he thought. 'This must be the unavoidable consequence of high status and power. It's just how things are; women were not made to be trusted.'

As though relieved of any guilt, his good humour and appetite returned and, when his brother came back from the hunt, he found Shahzenan looking relaxed and cheerful.

'What has changed your mood, dear Brother?' asked Shahriar. 'You have seemed so distressed since you came. I was worried about you.'

Then Shahzenan told his brother how he had discovered the plot against himself in Tartary, which his own beloved wife had instigated, and how he had killed her and all the conspirators.

Shahriar listened in horror. 'My dear Brother, no wonder you were so melancholic! But tell me, what has brought about your change of mood?'

At first, Shahzenan was reluctant to tell his brother that his own wife too was being disloyal, but after much pleading he said, 'The reason I am no longer afflicted by anger is because I've come to the conclusion that it is in the nature of all women to be treacherous, not just our wives. We men must be on our guard and not take their fidelity for granted.' And he told Shahriar what he had overheard.

'What, my wife too?' Shahriar fell into an uncontrollable rage, and immediately gave instructions for his wife and her fellow conspirators to be put to the sword.

Soon after, Shahzenan said his farewells and set off home for Tartary.

Now it was his brother, Shahriar, who was thrown into deep bitterness and melancholy. So King Shahriar came to a vengeful decision. To avoid any further disloyalty, he would marry a different maiden every day, and every next morning she would be executed. He summoned his counsellors and instructed them to put this cruel law into effect immediately.

The decree caused consternation throughout the city. Fathers and mothers gazed upon their daughters with terror, for even as they heard the news, a maiden was married one day and strangled the next. The kingdom was filled with tears and lamentation and, very quickly, instead of their King being someone they revered and loved, he became an object of dread. Every day, the shocked and reluctant vizier was forced to obtain a maiden for the King, knowing he was taking her to her death.

Now this vizier also had two daughters: the elder called Scheherazade, and the younger, Dinasarde. Both were highly accomplished: Scheherazade excelled in philosophy, medicine and history, and loved poetry and the arts, and Dinasarde who, above all, loved reading and storytelling, was one of the best writers of her time. Both were maidens of great virtue with unsurpassed beauty. But Scheherazade could see the distress and the anguish which her father, the vizier, was suffering as, every day, he had to find another maiden for the King and listen to the cries of another family filling the air.

One day, while the vizier and Scheherazade walked in the garden in deep melancholy, for laughter had not been heard anywhere since this terrible decree, Scheherazade said, 'Father, I have a request to make.'

'My child, I will grant you anything within reason,' he replied lovingly.

'I want to stop this barbarity that is afflicting the kingdom. Take me to the King tomorrow. Let me be his next bride.'

The vizier was appalled at such a notion. 'Never, never! As long as I have breath I will protect you from this insanity. Do you really expect me to be the executioner of my own daughter? Never, never!'

But Scheherazade persisted. 'Dear Father, if you don't take me to the King, I will go alone and offer myself to him. Let me try and stop the killing, and if I fail, I will at least have died with honour.'

At last the vizier consented and went instantly to Shahriar and told the King he would be bringing his own daughter in marriage the next day.

The King was surprised. 'Why are you making this sacrifice? You do realize that if I marry your daughter, she won't be exempt from my decree? I will expect you to put her to death the next morning, and if you do not, your own life will be forfeit.'

'It is what she desires,' replied the vizier with a breaking heart. When the King agreed, the vizier returned to his daughter and said she would have her wish.

'Dearest Father, I hope my plan will succeed and that you will never have cause to repent of this deed.' Then she went and dressed herself as a bride, in her richest of silks and jewellery, and prepared for her wedding day.

Before she left, Scheherazade went to her sister, Dinasarde, who was weeping at the certain fate of her sister. 'I beg you, dear Sister,' said Scheherazade, 'I have one request which I hope you will grant me. Before dawn tomorrow, I shall ask for you to be summoned to the King's chamber, and you must beg me to tell you one of those entertaining stories which you and I have shared so often.'

Dinasarde was only too pleased to comply, but wondered at this request.

That evening, the King lifted the veil from Scheherazade's face and was amazed by her beauty, and charmed by her manner and intelligence. But he noticed tears in her eyes, and was moved to ask what he could do, though her death at dawn was irrevocable.

'Sire,' replied Scheherazade, 'I have a sister, who loves me dearly. Please may she come and see me one last time tomorrow morning before dawn?'

The King agreed, and so the next morning, before dawn, Dinasarde entered the King's chamber where her sister awaited her calmly and sweetly.

After they embraced, Dinasarde said, 'Oh dearest Sister! What I shall miss most are the wonderful stories you tell me. I beseech you, tell me one last story before you are taken into paradise.'

The King gave his permission but said, 'You'd better hurry, Scheherazade, as you must die at dawn.'

So Scheherazade began a story which her sister, Dinasarde, had told her earlier, and which was called *The Enchanted Horse*.

The Enchanted Horse

The sorcerer was dreaming. Dreams as dark as swirling ink blobs creating extraordinary creatures: half bird, half fish; half ass, half crocodile; half hyena, half lizard, with open jaws and lunging claws. Suddenly … the sorcerer sat up, half awake, half asleep, unwilling to lose his vision. His long scaly fingers stretched in front of him, shaping an object in the air. With eyes still closed, he slid from his bed, his fingers still adding details to the thing. At last, he opened his eyes; wide awake now, he gasped with satisfaction. There before him stood a horse.

With quiet joy he examined his creation. He felt its legs, patted its body, lifted its hooves, smoothed out its mane, stared into its mouth, and stretched its tail. But this horse was not a living horse, though it had all the attributes of a real horse. It was a mechanical horse, with knobs and levers and something else very special; something which definitely made it a suitable gift for a Caliph who was, that very day, celebrating the festival of Norooz.

Ever since dawn, the Persian court had been awake preparing for the celebrations. Slaves cleaned, swept and dusted the palace courtyard, and polished the tiles round the minarets. Among them strode an overseer with whip in hand, checking, urging, and bullying them. The sun rose higher and the people of the city gathered expectantly. Dancers, musicians, jugglers, acrobats, fire-eaters and clowns arrived and entertained the waiting crowds. Then a wail of clarinets, an ear-splitting blast of horns, and a rattle of drums announced the arrival of the Caliph. The crowds surged forward to see the spectacle.

A long military procession wound through the gate in full uniform, their long robes swaying as they marched in a swinging rhythmical beat led by their major-domo strutting in front. They were followed by the cavalry with gleaming scimitars at their sides, spears in their hands, astride shining horses, proudly clip-clopping, with polished brasses, and decorated bridles. Dancing girls twirled, bearing baskets of rose petals which they scattered before the palanquin bearing the Caliph's daughter. The princess peeped secretively from behind wafting muslin curtains. Riding alongside was her brother, Prince Feroze Shah, upright and proud on his battle horse, wearing full regal dress, with a plumed emerald-green turban on his head, and a purple robe stitched with gold which glittered in the sunlight.

The palanquin was set down beneath the shade of a lemon tree, and brother and sister waited. Finally, with an ear-splitting blast of trumpets and beating of drums, the Caliph entered. How splendid he looked, riding high on the back of a giant elephant, seated in a howdah of gold and scarlet, with velvet drapes and cushions. A slave fanned him with peacock feathers, while others offered him dishes of fruit and water. Warriors with spears ran alongside.

In the centre of the grand courtyard, the elephant stopped and then slowly and smoothly lowered itself to a sitting position, and the Caliph settled to watch the entertainment which had been prepared for him.

The dancers danced, the musicians played, the acrobats tumbled and cartwheeled and, with heart-stopping skill, formed a towering pyramid one on top of the other. A line of distinguished guests appeared carrying gifts. One by one, they placed their Norooz presents into the keeping of the elephant's trunk which was then lifted up to the Caliph, who expressed his thanks with a wave of his royal hand.

Shuffling closer and closer was the sorcerer leading his horse. He cut a strange figure in his peculiar, somewhat shabby robes, not in the least like an honoured guest.

'Where is your gift?' asked the major-domo.

'Here,' replied the sorcerer curtly, indicating his horse.

'Why would His Gracious Majesty want another horse,' sneered the major-domo, 'when he has a hundred of the best horses in his stable? Were you invited to the party?' he asked suspiciously.

'What's going on?' demanded the Caliph, looking down.

'Some fellow desires to give you a horse, Your Graciousness, though I suspect he is an interloper.'

'Take him away then,' commanded the Caliph. 'Have him whipped.'

As the major-domo gripped the sorcerer by the collar, the sorcerer called out, 'Ah, but Your Majesty, this is no ordinary horse. This is a flying horse.'

The major-domo stopped and laughed with disbelief, then tried to continue dragging him away.

'Let me demonstrate it!' yelled the sorcerer.

'Stop!' The Caliph was curious. 'A flying horse? Show me.' He pointed to a huge mountain three leagues away. 'Go and fetch me the branch of a palm tree that grows on the peak. But I warn you, if you are trying to make a fool out of me I'll have your head cut off!'

Triumphantly, the sorcerer shook himself free of the major-domo, and mounted his horse. There was an expectant hush. Everyone turned to look;

the man must be mad. But, cool as a cucumber, he leaned forward and secretly twisted a peg under the horse's mane. The horse reared up on its hind legs, and lo, all four feet left the ground. The horse was flying! Up, up, and up, it flew; higher than the city walls, higher than the minarets, till it was just a speck in the sky flying towards the mountain.

The Caliph shaded his eyes; the princess, unable to resist, lifted aside her curtains to see. Prince Feroze Shah was open-mouthed with astonishment, and the people craned their necks till the sorcerer and his horse were no longer in sight.

Just when they wondered whether the sorcerer would return, they saw the speck coming back into view. Closer, closer, down, down, down he came and landed as lightly as a feather in front of the Caliph's elephant, bearing the branch of a palm tree.

'Your Highness,' he said, offering up the palm.

'I certainly accept this horse!' exclaimed the Caliph. 'It's wonderful!'

'Ah!' said the sorcerer. 'I'm afraid I demand something in exchange.'

'Why yes, of course!' The Caliph threw him a
bag of gold.

The sorcerer shook his head and refused it. The
Caliph threw him another and another, but still the
sorcerer rejected the payment.

'I must have this horse,' declared the Caliph passionately. 'What is it you desire? You can have anything you wish: elephants, titles, palaces, slaves? Name your desires.'

'Anything?' repeated the sorcerer?
'Is that a promise?'

'On my word as a king, I promise,' declared the Caliph impetuously.

The sorcerer looked triumphantly towards the princess, peeping through the muslin curtains of her palanquin. She fell back in horror, immediately predicting what the sorcerer would desire.

'The flying horse is yours, Your Excellency, in exchange for the hand in marriage of your daughter, the princess.'

At first, everybody rocked with merriment. What a thought. This man, a trickster no doubt, marrying the princess? Ha, ha, ha!

'You gave me a king's promise,' the sorcerer reminded him.

The Caliph fell back among his cushions, realizing he had been tricked. 'No, no, anything but that!' he cried in despair. But the sorcerer was adamant.

'No!' murmured the crowd in horror as
word spread.

The Caliph gazed at the horse and stroked
his beard. He leaned forward hesitantly. How he
wanted that horse. A terrible cry echoed round
the palace. 'No! Surely the Caliph won't give his
daughter away in exchange for the horse – even a
horse that can fly?'

Prince Feroze Shah spurred his horse towards
his sister. He pulled aside the muslin curtain and
clasped her hand. 'Dear Sister, don't worry, I'll
never let this creature have you.' He drew his
sword defensively.

The sorcerer smiled at the prince and spread his
hands. 'Why, Your Most Immeasurable Highness! At
least try my horse,' he entreated. 'Come, come; a
little ride!' His voice oozed like honey.

The prince backed away. 'No!' But he was
beguiled; he was enchanted by the horse; he
longed to ride it. He went forward.

'No, Brother!' whispered the princess.

'Yes?' murmured the sorcerer.

Prince Feroze Shah dismounted from his horse. 'I'll just take a look,' he said, approaching the strange horse which stood as static as a piece of wood.

'Try it, try it!' The sorcerer whispered like a summer wind.

The courtyard was silent; everyone held their breath. Only the princess's plaintive voice called out, 'No, Brother, no!'

But it was too late. Unable to resist, Prince Feroze Shah mounted the sorcerer's horse.

It didn't move a muscle. 'How do I make it fly?' he demanded.

'Here!' The sorcerer showed him the peg hidden in the horse's mane. 'Pull it forwards.'

The prince pulled it. The horse quivered, and at the speed of lightning, rose into the air and was away. The crowd surged forward, heads upturned, mouths open with amazement. The Caliph gasped. Only the princess held her head in her hands, full of dismay.

Prince Feroze Shah rose higher and higher, higher

than the tallest minaret, higher than the eagle circling above. So high, that the earth was just a pale orb below. Silvery stars glimmered around him as the sun dipped towards the horizon.

'It's time he came back.' The Caliph was anxious. 'Why isn't he coming down? Night is falling!'

The sorcerer shrugged apologetically.

'Bring him down, I say!' yelled the Caliph.

'I can't,' replied the sorcerer. 'Only he can bring himself down.'

'How?' demanded the Caliph.

'By pulling the down lever.'

'Did you tell him where the down lever is?' asked the Caliph.

'He didn't ask me, and I had no time to tell him – he flew away so fast,' said the sorcerer.

The Caliph howled with rage. 'Guards! Arrest this man. Throw him in my deepest dungeon!' The guards surrounded the sorcerer, thrusting spears around him like a cage. 'You will stay there until my son returns,' roared the Caliph. He stared with anguish up into the darkening sky.

High among the glittering stars, and beginning
to feel hungry, Prince Feroze Shah tried to make the
horse return. He knew that if there was a lever which
took him up, there must be one that would bring
him down. All night long, he twisted this way and
that, feeling under the bridle and saddle. At last, he
felt under the tail. It was there! He pulled it. To his
joy, the horse started to descend. But where would
he land: in desert, jungle, or mountain range?

Then, appearing out of the dawn mist, an exotic

place of rivers and forests appeared and, gleaming
in the darkness, was a magnificent palace. The
horse floated down and landed on a marble
terrace, with balustrades and steps leading to
further terraces. The prince dismounted. He looked
around. Whose kingdom had he come to? He saw a
staircase and cautiously descended. It led him to a
half-open door. He stepped quietly inside.

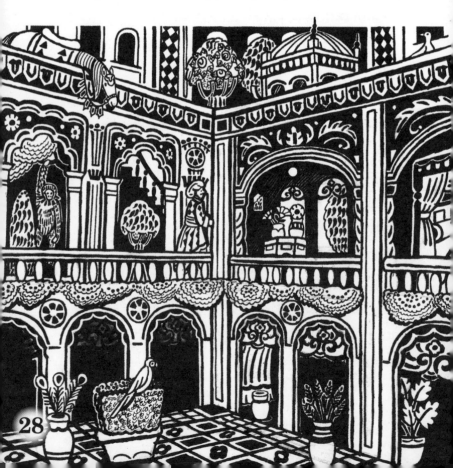

His heart almost stopped with wonder. He had entered a bedchamber, and there lay a sleeping maiden, more beautiful than any woman he had ever seen, and so richly attired there was no question that she must be a princess. He knelt by her side full of awe and touched her hand. Her eyes flew open and she sat up in astonishment, pulling a gauze drape across her face to veil herself from this stranger.

'Don't be afraid,' murmured the prince, bowing his head respectfully. 'I am Prince Feroze Shah, son of the Caliph of Persia. By some amazing adventure of enchantment, I have been brought here and kneel now at your side and beg for your help and protection.'

The lady immediately saw the goodness and nobility in the face of this young prince, and was not afraid. 'I am the eldest daughter of the Rajah of Bengal,' she said. 'My father keeps me in this palace away from all harm. But I assure you this is not a barbarous country. I offer you all my protection and hospitality.'

And she clapped her hands to awaken her handmaidens, and ordered them to prepare a chamber for the prince to sleep in, and to make sure he was given dishes of the finest food and fruit. 'I will restrain my curiosity till the morning to know by what wondrous means you have arrived at my palace, and managed to evade the vigilance of my guards,' she told the prince.

The next morning, the Princess of Bengal took extra care of her appearance: she beautified her face in the mirror, her handmaidens combed and oiled her hair, then plaited it with diamonds. She put on robes of silk in colours of turquoise and pink and purple and green, and glittering jewellery adorned her neck, and ears, and wrists, and fingers and toes.

Then she sent a message to the prince announcing her willingness to meet him.

When they met, they were like two wonderful birds exchanging compliments, each admiring the other, and each falling in love with the other as the prince told her about his adventures. 'But Madam,' he said respectfully, after some time had passed. 'I must go straight away back home to my kingdom, so that I can return in a manner befitting a prince, to ask your father for your hand in marriage.'

The princess clapped her hands with joy to hear of his love, but said, 'Oh fair prince, you cannot leave me so soon. It will cast me into the deepest misery to see you go. Stay awhile: tell me about your adventures; tell me about the royal court of Persia.'

Although Prince Feroze Shah was anxious to get home and reassure everyone that he was safe and well, he could hardly refuse the request of the princess who had shown him such hospitality. And so he stayed and, while he told her of his adventures, and what life was like back home in the royal Persian court, she beguiled him with every enchantment.

Two months went by when again, the prince pleaded to be allowed to go home. 'Madam, I really can stay no longer. My father will be so worried, but I promise to return to you as soon as possible.'

The princess looked so downhearted that he said,

'Madam, I fear you may be offended by a suggestion I have, but … '

She looked up expectantly, with moist eyes.

'Come with me. Come with me to my home in Persia. Meet my father. There is room for us both on the magic horse.'

Her face flushed with excitement, then paled at the thought of how angry her father would be. He would never give his permission, and she was guarded closely night and day. Then suddenly, her fears gave way to determination. 'We must leave secretly,' she whispered. 'Let us meet tomorrow just before dawn while all my attendants are asleep.'

'I'll be waiting for you on the upper terrace with the horse,' agreed the prince.

The sky was still black, and stars still glittered like silvery fish caught in the net of night. The horse stood silent and still, as the prince hung anxiously in the shadows waiting for the princess.

Suddenly, there was a rustle of silk, and a waft of perfume, and there she was. With great tenderness, he lifted her up onto the horse, then leaped on himself and took the reins. She clasped her arms round his waist. 'Are you sure you can control this magical creature?' she asked.

'I'm sure,' he whispered, and turned the peg beneath the horse's mane.

The horse sprang into the air. With the smoothness and lightness of a feather, they ascended up and up, into the stars leaving the land of Bengal and, before even the first rose of dawn tinged the sky, there below was the kingdom of Persia.

'Madam,' said the prince. 'It would be more fitting if I take you first to a

small palace not far from the city where you can refresh yourself, and I can go ahead and prepare my father for your arrival.'

It was a beautiful palace: all fitted with carpets and divans, and many servants to attend to her every need. Here, he left her and, assuring her of his swift return, Prince Feroze Shah leaped on the horse again and, in a second, was standing before his astonished father, the Caliph.

Of course the happiness at the safe return of Prince Feroze Shah was beyond bounds and his sister, too, wept for joy. Being an honourable man, the Caliph immediately sent for his prisoner, the sorcerer.

'I said you must be my prisoner until my son had safely returned,' said the Caliph. 'Well, now he has. So take your horse and leave my kingdom, and never show your face here again.'

But all the while he had been in prison, the sorcerer had been plotting revenge. By means of his magic powers, he knew where the Princess of Bengal was waiting. Now that he was at liberty, he jumped on his horse and flew directly there. How easily he gained entrance past the gatekeeper, how easily he bowed before the princess and spoke with courtesy and reassurance. 'I have been sent by the Caliph to accompany Your Highness to the palace where he is waiting to receive you with his son, Prince Feroze Shah.' So plausible was he that the princess had no hesitation in agreeing to go with him.

With what glee the sorcerer helped the princess onto the enchanted horse, and leaping in front of her, turned the peg, and up they rose into the air.

'Where are you taking me?' screamed the Princess of Bengal, as she saw they were flying in the wrong direction.

'To my home in Kashmir, where you must agree to become my wife,' cried the magician triumphantly, flying towards the east. In barely a wink of an eye, the horse set them down near a beautiful lake, with silvery fish leaping, and banks abounding with fruit trees and flowers, where birds of exquisite colours and plumage strutted and flew. 'Give up thoughts of Persia,' murmured the magician in an oily voice. 'Marry me now. This place of paradise will be your home.'

'Never, never!' wept the princess. 'I shall never marry you.'

The magician roared with fury, and gripped the princess violently, hurting her so much she screamed for help. At that moment, the Sultan of Kashmir, who happened to be out hunting, heard her cries and came to see what he could do to help.

'She is my wife!' protested the magician. 'And I can do what I like with her.'

The princess fell to her knees before the Sultan. 'Whoever you are, you who the heavens have sent to save me, I beg you, don't listen to this man. He is an imposter and a liar. I am betrothed to the Prince of Persia, and this foul creature has abducted me.'

The Sultan of Kashmir listened to her story with increasing anger, and knew it to be true. So without any further ado he cried, 'Guards! Take him away and put him in chains!' They did so immediately.

The princess was overjoyed to be freed from her abductor. She was certain that her deliverer would now enable her to return to Persia. But the Sultan of Kashmir, hardly able to believe his luck in coming across so beautiful a princess, decided to marry her himself. He ordered the kingdom to commence the celebrations and prepare for a magnificent wedding with beating drums, blasting trumpets and plucking strings.

On seeing her fortunes take yet another dreadful twist, the princess fainted away.

Back in Persia, there had been rejoicing that the prince had returned, and with a princess he wished to marry. The Caliph himself had decided to come with his entourage to greet the Princess of Bengal, and Prince Feroze Shah was already galloping ahead to prepare her. But the guards and courtiers had fallen into terrified confusion at the sight of him. 'Why, Sire! She has already gone. Did you not send a messenger to escort her to the Caliph's palace?'

'Gone? Who took her? Which way did they go?' cried the prince in horror.

But then the prince knew; it could only be the sorcerer. Utterly broken-hearted, the prince decided to set out across the world in search of his princess. Disguising himself as a wandering disciple he set forth, uncertain which way to go, but declaring, 'I shall find my princess, or die in the attempt.'

'Sister!' Dinasarde murmured fearfully. 'See, the dawn!'

Scheherazade stopped her storytelling, and saw through the window the first blush of daylight spreading across the night sky.

'Why have you stopped?' demanded the King, Shahriar. 'What happened next?'

'Sire,' said Scheherazade gently. 'It is dawn and I

must die. That is your decree.'

'That's true, I suppose,' the King blustered. 'But I have to know the outcome of this story. I must know what happened. Did the prince find her?'

Scheherazade shrugged.

'Very well,' growled the King. 'I'll make an exception just this once. Come back tomorrow night and finish the story. Your execution can wait a day.'

That day, the King could hardly deal with his duties of state, so anxious was he to hear the rest of the story, and as night fell, he went to his chamber and waited impatiently for the return of the beautiful Scheherazade.

For a second night, Scheherazade came to her husband, the King. And though he was again enchanted by her beauty and intelligence, he was desperate to know how the story would end. Knowing that she must die at dawn, he urged her to continue.

'Very well,' smiled Scheherazade, settling herself among the silken cushions.

For many days, weeks and months, Prince Feroze Shah travelled from town to town, from one province to another and one country to another. Everywhere he went he asked if anyone had seen a princess from Bengal, till grief and fatigue wore him down, and he knew not which way to go.

One day, while resting in a certain town in Hindustan, he overheard gossip about a princess who was supposed to be marrying the Sultan of Kashmir, but who had suddenly gone mad on the day of the wedding. Physicians had been summoned from all over the world to find a cure for her, but none had succeeded.

There was something about the story which made the prince curious and, very soon, he was hastening towards the kingdom of Kashmir. He took lodging not far from the Sultan's palace, and heard more of this mad princess. They said she had arrived in the kingdom on a horse, in the company of a magician who had claimed to be her husband, but who was not. The Sultan had ordered him to be thrown into prison and was about to marry the princess himself, when she had suddenly gone mad.

'She shrieks strange words, and throws herself about violently; she tears her hair, and whirls round and round till she falls to the ground, then crawls like an animal, uttering odd noises,' people told him. 'Why, she's even attacked the Sultan himself. He is distraught, and has summoned many physicians, but none has been able to help and, if any attempts to come near, she just throws herself into a frenzy and won't let them approach her.'

Prince Feroze Shah was determined to see this princess for himself and, to this end, disguised himself as a physician. He sent word to the Sultan, that he was a learned physician from a far country who had heard of the princess's illness. Having exceptional knowledge, he wanted to offer his services in the hope of finding a cure for her. The Sultan, who had despaired of there being any cure, was only too glad to allow this learned doctor to enter the palace. He had him taken immediately to the princess's chamber, though he warned him that the princess loathed the sight of doctors, and just one glimpse was enough to make her ferociously agitated.

The prince asked first to be able to spy on her secretly, and was taken to a lattice window where he was able to view her without being seen. There he beheld his beloved princess, sitting so quietly, rocking gently with grief as she sang a song bewailing her fate.

The prince went straight to the Sultan and told him he was sure he could cure her. 'But you must let me have an audience with her completely alone.'

The Sultan agreed, and soon Prince Feroze Shah was let into her chamber.

When she saw his physician's garb, she flew into a rage and began screaming. But he went close up to her and whispered in her ear, 'Hush, princess! I am not a physician. It is I, Prince Feroze Shah, and I have come to rescue you.'

She stared in amazement at this man whose beard had grown long, and who looked so strange in his disguise. But she knew his voice, and a great joy leaped into her heart and she trembled with excitement. 'I'm not really mad,' she assured him. 'I'm only pretending. It's the only way I can think of to keep the Sultan from marrying me.'

'Where is the sorcerer's horse?' asked the prince. 'It could help us to escape.'

'The Sultan of Kashmir kept it because he knows it's enchanted. But he has no idea how it works,' said the princess. 'It stands in the palace square.'

'Ah!' said the prince. 'Then I have an idea. Be calm and do as I say.'

The prince then went to see the Sultan, and told him that, although he had managed to calm the princess, he needed to do more. 'Can Your Highness tell me in what manner the princess arrived in your country?'

'She came on a horse which people said was enchanted because it isn't a living horse. That's why I kept it, though no one knows how the enchantment works.'

'Ah!' said the prince. 'Nonetheless, I think the enchantment of the horse has rubbed off on the princess, and is responsible for her madness. Please have the princess dressed in her most luxurious clothes, and fabulous jewels, and bring her to the horse in the town square.'

The Sultan agreed. Word spread quickly that the princess was to be brought to the horse. Crowds gathered in the town square, believing they were about to witness something extraordinary, and they waited excitedly for the princess to arrive.

A gasp rippled through the crowd. There she was. Never had she looked more beautiful, dressed in her finest silks and adorned with jewels, yet behaving madly, giving raucous shrieks, and flinging her arms about. Then the prince appeared, still disguised as a physician. He placed a flickering charcoal burner on the ground nearby then lifted the princess onto the horse's back. Now, solemnly

folding his hands across his chest, he walked three times round the horse, muttering incantations, and sprinkling dust over the charcoal burner causing it to spit and sparkle.

A hush fell over the crowd. The Sultan leaned forward with anticipation. What would happen now? With a flourish, the prince dug his hand into another pocket and, raising his closed fist above the red coals, opened his fingers, then with a loud cry, let fall a stream of powder. There was a spurt of fire; a billow of smoke enveloped both the princess and the prince. No one saw him leap onto the horse, but everyone heard the words he shouted to the Sultan: 'When you would marry a princess who has implored your protection, learn first to obtain her permission,' and with that he twisted the peg under the mane, and the horse rose into the air. In the twinkling of an eye, it had gone, and so had the Prince of Persia and his Bengal princess – back to the kingdom of the Caliph, who ordered ten days of rejoicing at the miraculous return of his son.

'See what you did?' shrieked a terrible voice from the crowd. 'That was my horse, and I could have killed the prince had you not thrown me into prison.'

The Sultan of Kashmir turned to see the sorcerer somehow free of his chains, raging at the back of the crowd. 'But I know where to go to get more powers,' said the sorcerer. 'If I can't have my flying horse, then I must have a princess of my own.' And before anyone could take action, he vanished.

Aladdin and the Magic Lamp

Without his horse, or a princess, the wicked sorcerer plotted to gain more powers and take revenge. *If I could get hold of the powers of the genii, then no one in the world would be able to challenge me*, he thought, for he had heard of a place where a genie dwelled. But because of a curse, he could only gain the power of this genie with the help of another person. So it was for this purpose that the sorcerer first made his way to the land of Cathay, looking for someone who could help him. He wandered for some time until one day, while passing through a small town on the edge of a desert, he overheard a woman chastising her son for being a lazy good-for-nothing. Her angry voice came from a simple tailor's shop. A young lad came rushing out with his mother in pursuit, who lashed about him with a stick.

'You bad boy! You useless good-for-nothing! Call yourself my son?' his mother raged. But he only laughed and leaped out of her way.

'Get out of my sight,' she shouted. 'I've a good mind to send you packing for good.'

'You wouldn't do that!' laughed the boy. 'You love me too much!' And he skipped away to join his friends in the street.

The sorcerer followed the lad, and observed him closely.

'This boy,' he thought, 'is just the sort of boy I'm looking for.' The sorcerer saw his bright, intelligent face, and his strong body. He made some discreet enquiries round the neighbourhood, and learned that the boy was called Aladdin, and was the son of a tailor, Mustapha, who had sadly died. People shook their heads disapprovingly, telling the sorcerer that unlike his hard-working father, Aladdin was lazy and a trial to his mother.

'Boy!' The sorcerer beckoned the boy to come over. 'Are you Aladdin, son of the tailor, Mustapha?'

'I am indeed, Sir,' replied the boy.

Then the sorcerer flung his arms round him in a hearty embrace. 'Why then, you are my nephew, for I am your father's long-lost brother.'

'Really?' cried Aladdin with astonishment. 'I didn't know I had an uncle. I must tell my mother.'

'Here, take this for her,' said the sorcerer, pushing some gold coins into Aladdin's pocket, 'and tell her I shall come for supper tonight.'

Aladdin rushed home excitedly. 'My uncle is in town. Why didn't you tell me I had an uncle?'

But his mother said, 'Your father did once have a brother, but he died. No, Son, you have no uncle on either my side or your father's.'

'Well, he's coming for supper, and look what he gave me.' He took a handful of gold coins out of his pocket. 'Now you can go and buy food and cook him a feast.'

Wonderingly, the poor woman went to the market and bought lots of fine food, and prepared a royal supper of breads, dates, apricot and grape juice, and choicest sweetmeats. Then they waited. 'Perhaps he won't find his way,' murmured Aladdin's mother.

'Hmm,' murmured Aladdin uncertainly, 'I'm starving.' He was just about to begin eating, when the sorcerer arrived loaded with gifts.

He knelt at the feet of Aladdin's mother, kissed them and wept. 'Oh, how sorry I am not to have found you sooner. My poor, poor brother! How I miss him. How you must miss him too. Pray, show me the sofa on which he used to sit; show me the bed in which he used to sleep, and the table at which he used to eat.' At each place, he knelt and prayed and wept with deep sorrow. 'I have been travelling the world,' he said. 'Forty years it is, since I went away, and now I return to find my brother is no more. But this fine boy,' and he drew Aladdin to his side, 'what a comfort and support this boy must be to you, Madam,' he said.

Aladdin shuffled uncomfortably, knowing what a bad son he had been, and his mother bowed her head in shame. 'Ever since his father died, I have tried to make Aladdin become more responsible, and help me in the trade of tailoring,' she said. 'But alas, he is so lazy – you can see for yourself what an idle lad he is. I've been thinking of throwing him out.'

'Oh dear, dear, dear!' sighed the sorcerer. 'Well, let's see about that. I shall come again tomorrow and take the boy, and get him started in life. It's the least I can do in memory of my brother.'

So the sorcerer came the next day; he had Aladdin dressed in fine clothes, then escorted him round the town to meet merchants and shopkeepers, to teach him how a business should be run. He showed Aladdin fine houses and palaces, and said, 'Why, one day, you too could live in such places, if you make a success of your business – which I shall set you up in!' Aladdin was much impressed, and his mother overjoyed. After that, the sorcerer came almost every day, showing Aladdin more and more, and always pressing gold coins in his hand for his mother.

Then one day, the sorcerer took Aladdin out into the countryside beyond the city walls. They walked a long way till they reached a valley between two mountains. After a while, in that lonely place, they stopped, and the sorcerer ordered Aladdin to gather sticks for a fire. The magician then lit the sticks and, when the fire was burning merrily, he suddenly

sprinkled some powder onto the flames and uttered strange words. At that moment, the earth trembled and, to Aladdin's consternation, the ground opened to reveal a stone with a brass ring. What kind of man was this? Filled with terror, Aladdin tried to run away, but the sorcerer grabbed him roughly, and boxed his ears.

'Ow, ow! Why did you do that?' wept Aladdin. 'What have I done to deserve such a beating?'

'I'm only doing what a father should do. Why did you run away?' And the sorcerer beat him again. Then he softened and said, 'My dear boy! If you just obey me without question, you will get undreamed-of rewards. All I ask is that you pull the ring in this stone. You see, it is a magic stone, and only you can lift it. But underneath is a treasure destined to be yours, and which will make you richer than any monarch in the whole wide world.'

Aladdin obeyed, and took hold of the ring. He pulled, and easily raised the stone to reveal a hole in the ground with steps descending into the darkness of a cave.

'Ah!' The sorcerer sighed with satisfaction. 'Now, you must do exactly what I tell you,' he told Aladdin. 'Go down these steps and you will come to three caves through which you must pass. Wrap your clothes tightly round you, for on no account must you touch the sides of the walls or you will die. In each cave are four large cisterns full of gold and silver. But whatever you do, don't touch them. Pass quickly through the caves until at the end of the third cave, you will come to a door. Open it and step outside into a garden. On the terrace, you will find a lamp. Empty it of oil, tuck it in your girdle and bring it to me.' Then the sorcerer took off a ring and put it on Aladdin's finger. 'It is a talisman, and will bring you good luck,' he explained.

Aladdin descended the steps and, remembering the sorcerer's words, moved quickly and carefully through the caves without touching anything. At the far end of the third cave, he opened the door. Just as he had been told, he found himself in a garden of fountains and flowers, winding paths and fruit trees full of the most glorious fruit. At first, he thought the fruits were oranges, lemons, apricots, pomegranates and plums. But, with astonishment he realized they were in fact precious stones of every hue. The sorcerer had said nothing about not touching those, so while preferring them to have been real fruit so that he could have eaten to assuage his hunger and quench his thirst, he stuffed his pockets and the seams of his garments with the jewels, then turned to find the lamp.

There it was, as the magician had said, standing on the terrace.

It was a dusty, ugly thing, and he couldn't imagine why his uncle wanted such an object but, following instructions, he emptied it of oil and carried it back through the three caves till he reached the steps.

With great difficulty he began his ascent, weighed down with jewels. When he reached the opening at the top, he shouted to his uncle to help him out.

'First give me the lamp,' cried the magician, for it was only the lamp he wanted, and he had planned to leave Aladdin in the cave for ever.

'I need a hand,' Aladdin pleaded. 'I can't give you the lamp till I am out.'

'Give it to me, give it to me,' shrieked the sorcerer, in a sudden fury. 'I order you!'

'Help me out, then!' cried Aladdin.

'Aaaaah!' screamed the sorcerer, his rage getting the better of him, and he flung some of his magic powder onto the fire. Immediately the stone slid back into place, trapping Aladdin inside.

'Grrrr!' roared the sorcerer, aghast at his own folly, and went shrieking back across the desert to Africa like a sandstorm.

'Let me out, let me out!' yelled Aladdin. But his voice could no more be heard from inside the cave than the high squeal of an eagle circling above. 'Let me out!' he wept, trying desperately to push the stone away, but to no avail. Terrified of the darkness, Aladdin resolved to return to the garden door. But when he turned the knob, it too was locked. In despair he fell to his knees and wept. Must he die, buried alive in this cave? What was he to do? He clasped his hands together in prayer, beseeching

God to help him, and in doing so he rubbed the ring which the sorcerer had put on his finger. Immediately, a creature of frightful aspect rose from the ground, bigger and bigger, till his huge dreadful shape filled the space around him.

'I am the genie of the ring; your every wish is my command. Speak, Master, and I will obey.'

Almost fainting with fright, Aladdin managed to cry, 'Get me out of here!'

In an instant, Aladdin found himself outside the cave, exactly where he had arrived with the man who had claimed to be his uncle. Gasping with relief, he hurried home and collapsed on the threshold before his mother.

'Mother, fetch me some food. I'm dying of hunger,' he begged when he had recovered a little.

'But Son, we have no food. I was hoping that wretched so-called uncle of yours would come with more. Now, we have nothing. I can't understand why he went to all that trouble just to get this dirty lamp. Perhaps if I clean it up a bit, we could sell it.' And she began to rub it with a cloth.

But no sooner had she rubbed a little, than a vast shape arose around them, and a creature of hideous aspect filled the room. With a scream of horror, Aladdin's mother fainted away. This creature was far more vast and far more hideous than the genie of the ring.

A great voice spoke. 'I am the genie of the lamp. Your every wish is my command. Speak, Master, and I will obey.'

Aladdin spoke boldly. 'Bring us some food.'

Immediately, the genie produced a great platter of twelve silver dishes containing the most delicious meats and breads and fruits, and a large flagon of grape juice with two silver goblets. Then the genie disappeared.

Aladdin roused his mother and led her to the table laden with food fit for a king. 'Now we know why that wicked man wanted the lamp so much.'

'But please put that lamp away,' begged his mother. 'I never want to see that hideous creature again.' So Aladdin pushed it to the back of a cupboard.

For a while, Aladdin and his mother lived very well,

for every time they needed anything, Aladdin took one of the silver dishes and sold it in the town and in this way they prospered, with plenty to eat and new clothes to wear.

Then one day, an announcement was made throughout the city, ordering everyone to stay indoors, because the Emperor's daughter, Buddir-al-Budoor, was due to pass by on her way to the baths, and it was forbidden on pain of death for anyone to look upon her. But Aladdin had heard of the exceptional beauty of this princess, and he couldn't resist sneaking across to the baths and hiding behind the door through which she would pass.

He caught but a brief glimpse when she lifted her veil as she entered – but enough to know that everything he had heard was true. She was the most beautiful woman he had ever seen or imagined. Aladdin was utterly enchanted and fell instantly in love with her. He became obsessed with winning her hand in marriage, and told his mother that somehow he must marry this princess or die. She shook her head with exasperation. 'Silly boy!'

But Aladdin was in deadly earnest and racked his brains to achieve his purpose. Then he remembered his coat, and how he had stuffed it with jewels from the garden. He devised a plan. First he took a china bowl and filled it with some of the jewels.

Their brilliance of colour and purity was almost too dazzling to behold, and he covered them with a napkin. 'Now, Mother,' he said. 'Go to the Emperor's palace where, each day, he holds audience with his people, and when your turn comes, give him this bowl and tell him I wish to marry his daughter.'

So Aladdin's mother set off to try and get an audience with the Emperor. But many people had also gone that day and, by the time she had shuffled within view of the Emperor, the audience was over, and she had to return home with the jewels. Six times she made the attempt, every day trying to position herself to catch the eye of the Emperor, but each time she was jostled away.

However, the Emperor had noticed this modest woman coming every day carrying a china bowl covered with a napkin, and he was curious to know why she had come, and what she carried. So he ordered his grand vizier to bring her before him if she came the next day.

It was the seventh day and, as before, Aladdin's mother arrived at the palace carrying her china dish covered with a cloth. This time the grand vizier ushered her before the Emperor, where she prostrated herself.

'I have noticed you coming each day,' the Emperor said, 'and I am curious to know what is in the bowl covered by the napkin.'

'Sire, I have a gift for you from my son,' and she held out the china dish. Somewhat bemused, the Emperor took the dish and lifted the napkin. He had to blink several times from the blinding light which rose from the dish, and gasped at the sight of the most lustrous, sparkling jewels he had ever seen. 'My goodness,' he exclaimed to his vizier, 'there can't be an Emperor on earth wealthier than the man who has sent these as a gift.'

'My son wishes to marry your daughter,' said Aladdin's mother apologetically. 'I've told him he's mad, but he loves your daughter more than all the world, more than anything money can buy.'

'Hmmm,' pondered the Emperor, stroking his beard, and gazing again at the fabulous jewels. 'If my daughter is so valued, then surely it would be advisable to accept this suitor.'

Now the grand vizier had wanted his own son to marry the princess, and he was quite put out at the thought of this humble woman's son ruining his plans. So he advised the Emperor to wait three months before committing himself. 'I think we need more proof of this suitor's credentials. He is after all a total stranger and, if I may remind you, you once regarded my son favourably as a possible husband for the princess.'

So the Emperor said, 'Madam, your son shall have my daughter's hand if, in the meantime, we do not get a better offer. Come back in three months.'

Time went by, and no one was able to offer anything as magnificent and extraordinary as the basket of jewels Aladdin's mother had given him. But now the Emperor was very reluctant to give up his daughter to a mere tailor, and hoped the woman would not appear, as the end of the three months drew near.

But exactly when the three months were up, Aladdin once more sent his mother to the Emperor. On seeing the woman waiting patiently in her simple clothes, the Emperor whispered to his vizier, 'What shall I do? I have to keep my promise!'

'Ask her to bring you something so extraordinary that she would be unable to fulfil your wish,' the vizier advised. So the Emperor beckoned her over. 'Madam,' he said, 'I have every intention of keeping my promise as a good Emperor should, but I still need a little reassurance. Please send me forty gold basins filled to the brim with jewels and carried before me by forty black slaves and forty white slaves, all dressed magnificently.'

Aladdin's mother went home to tell her son the impossible request.

'No, Mother, it's not impossible,' murmured Aladdin. 'I can do more than that to win the princess. Fetch me the lamp.' His mother rummaged for it in the cupboard and set it before her son. She shrank back fearfully, as Aladdin rubbed the lamp with the end of his shirt. Immediately, a vast monstrous shape flowed from the spout and grew bigger and bigger till it filled the entire cottage.

'I am the genie of the lamp. Your every wish is my command. Speak, Master, and I will obey!' boomed a voice.

'Fetch me forty basins made of gold and filled to the brim with jewels. Send me forty black slaves and forty white slaves, all fabulously dressed with bejewelled girdles, and let them carry the basins two by two to the Emperor.' In an instant Aladdin's wish was granted, and soon a grand procession of slaves, carrying the golden basins brimming with jewels, passed along the streets towards the palace, with Aladdin's mother being carried among them.

On entering the palace, the black slaves and the white slaves knelt in a semicircle before the Emperor, their arms folded across their chests, and their heads bowed submissively, while yet again, Aladdin's mother prostrated herself before the Emperor. 'My son hopes that you are pleased to see your wish fulfilled,' she murmured.

'Why, my good woman!' exclaimed the Emperor, overcome with amazement. 'Please return to your son and tell him I am ready to welcome him with open arms.'

73

'Your Highness, Inestimable Majesty,' whispered the grand vizier desperately. 'I fear you are the victim of a trick or some kind of sorcery. Wait a while longer. Let me prove it.'

But the bedazzled Emperor was won over by the lavish wealth of this mysterious suitor and replied harshly, 'My good man, you had three months to find any kind of fault, and you have not succeeded. No, I am convinced. Tailor or no tailor, I can do no better than allow my daughter to marry this man.'

Aladdin was triumphant. So that he would make a suitable entrance before the Emperor, he summoned the genie again. 'I want to be bathed in a scented bath, and dressed in the most lavish clothes, with twenty slaves to attend me; I want a white horse with plaited mane and bejewelled bridle surpassing any of the Emperor's own horses; I want my mother dressed in the finest silks befitting a queen, with six slaves to attend her and a palanquin to carry her. Finally, I want ten purses with a thousand gold coins in each purse.'

When all was delivered, Aladdin mounted

the horse and rode through the streets alongside his mother's palanquin, to the Emperor's palace – tossing gold coins from his purses as he went. How wild with joy the people were. 'What a fine, handsome, generous prince this is – a worthy husband for our beloved princess.'

The Emperor wanted Aladdin to marry his daughter immediately, but Aladdin said, 'No! First I must build the most beautiful palace in the world for my bride. Would you grant me some land alongside yours?'

The Emperor didn't hesitate, though he wondered how many months if not years that would take. But when he opened his window the next morning, it was to behold a gleaming, domed palace built of the finest marble, encrusted with agate, jade and jasper, with walls of gold and silver, and a hall of twenty-four latticed windows decorated with diamonds and rubies. All this appeared overnight along with stables and horses, with grooms and slaves; it was amazing – astonishing – incredible!

At last, Aladdin and his mother walked along a

specially laid carpet all the way to the Emperor's palace to announce that Aladdin was ready to marry the princess. The Emperor heartily agreed and, with the sounds of the Emperor's finest musicians with trumpets, pipes and cymbals ringing over the city, Aladdin received his princess and took her back to his palace.

And so, Aladdin married the beautiful princess Buddir-al-Budoor, and for some years they lived in peace and great happiness. No one was more loved or more respected than Aladdin, for he never lost his modesty and courteous bearing despite his great wealth and power. Word spread far and wide, and in due course reached the ears of the wicked magician:

the same evil sorcerer who had pretended to be Aladdin's uncle, and abandoned him to his fate, entombed in the cave all those years ago. He had presumed Aladdin to be dead. But hearing about palaces appearing overnight, and a prince with seemingly unending wealth, the magician decided this sounded like the work of a genie. So he set off to go and see for himself.

As he drew nearer the city where Aladdin lived, he heard more and more stories about this wonderful prince, who never went out without purses of gold coins to throw to the people; who had built a marvellous palace overnight; and seemed able to perform the most amazing feats in the twinkling of an eye.

With grinding teeth, and mounting fury, the sorcerer was sure now that somehow Aladdin had survived his entombment, and was in possession of the magic lamp, with the all-powerful genie at his command. He was determined to hunt him out and destroy him.

Now Aladdin had gone on an eight-day hunting trip and, that day, the magician entered the city with a plan to bring about his destruction. He had bought some brand new shining copper lamps and arranged them in a large basket. Then the sorcerer wandered through the streets crying out, 'New lamps for old, new lamps for old!' How the people laughed and jeered. What kind of a madman was this, offering to exchange beautiful new shining lamps for old, oil-smeared, dusty ones? Children followed him, tugging at his robes, and taunting this strange fellow who had come from goodness knows where. But the magician drew nearer and nearer the palace walls, shouting even louder: 'New lamps for old, new

lamps for old. Bring me your worn and filthy lamps
and I will give you new ones to illumine your homes.'
The people laughed even louder, and their jeers and
taunts reached the ears of the princess sitting in her
hall of twenty-four windows.

'What's going on out there?' demanded the princess, and sent one of her handmaidens to investigate.

The girl came back laughing. 'Why Your Highness, it is the most ridiculous thing. A madman is offering to give away new lamps for old.'

Another handmaid said, 'There's a dusty old lamp sitting on a high shelf in that alcove. It must be pretty useless. Why not give him that and see what happens?' Neither she nor anyone knew that this was Aladdin's magic lamp which he had placed discreetly on a high shelf till he returned from hunting.

'Give it to him then!' cried the princess merrily. 'Make the exchange.'

So the handmaiden took the dusty old lamp from its shelf and went down to the palace gates. 'Hey, you! Here's an old lamp I'd like to exchange. Give me a new lamp for this!'

The magician, hardly able to disguise his glee, snatched the lamp from her hands and thrust in its place a copper one. Triumphantly, with the sound of jeers and taunts ringing in his ears, he hurried away from the city and out into the desert beyond, clutching Aladdin's lamp beneath his robes.

The sorcerer waited till nightfall before placing the lamp on a rock before him and rubbing it with his sleeve.

With a great whoosh, a dreadful creature rose up and up and up, and a terrible face loomed over him. 'I am the genie of the lamp. Your every wish is my command. Speak, Master, and I will obey.'

'Dispatch Aladdin's palace, his princess, slaves, and all who live within it to a lonely desert place in Africa,' ordered the magician with malicious joy, and in an instant, it was done.

If you remember, Aladdin had been away on an eight-day hunting trip and …

Scheherazade stopped abruptly. She gazed out of a window facing the east, and saw a faint crack in the night sky through which a grey light was

beginning to squeeze itself. 'It is time,' she whispered. 'The dawn is coming. My life must end now.'

'What?' cried King Shahriar, leaping from his bed. 'You can't stop now. You haven't finished the story. What happens next?'

She turned and looked at him sadly, and shrugged. 'It is your decree, My Lord, and must be obeyed.'

Shahriar huffed and puffed with frustration. He went to the window. Sure enough, night was ending and any moment now it would be sunrise. 'Oh!' huffed the King. 'Bother,' puffed the King. 'Well then,' he spluttered, 'as it was I who made the decree, I can do what I like. I give you another day to finish the story. Then you shall die. Come back tonight.'

Scheherazade bowed deeply, and stepping backwards to the door, was led away to live another day.

The next evening after sunset, Scheherazade was brought to the King's chamber. 'Good, good!' cried the King eagerly. 'Get on with the story. I want to know what happened next. What happened to Aladdin?'

So Scheherazade settled herself among the silk cushions and continued the story.

If you remember, Aladdin had been away on an eight-day hunting trip. He could not possibly have imagined the catastrophe that had taken place while he was away. That morning, the Emperor had opened his window as usual on awakening, to gaze with awe at Aladdin's palace which he could see at the far end of his gardens – but this time – there was nothing, absolutely nothing; not one tower, dome, window, horse, groom or slave.

The whole palace with everything in it had simply vanished. He rubbed his eyes, and shook his head in disbelief, but it was true. The palace had gone. He yelled for his grand vizier. 'Look!' he shouted. 'Where's the palace?'

The vizier was so astonished he was dumbstruck. He too rubbed his eyes and struck his head in case he was dreaming. 'I knew there was sorcery afoot,' he murmured. 'This man you gave in marriage to your daughter is a magician. He must be destroyed.'

The Emperor agreed, and sent soldiers to apprehend Aladdin who was on his way back from the hunt. They soon came across him and dragged him from his horse like a common criminal. Then, forcing him to run before them, they whipped him through the city streets to the palace. The citizens were outraged. 'How dare you treat our beloved Aladdin in this way?' they bellowed, and a huge crowd accompanied the prisoner as he was dragged inside the palace gates.

'Fetch the executioner!' demanded the Emperor, as Aladdin was thrown before him. 'Off with his head.'

The executioner bound Aladdin's eyes with a blindfold, forced him to bow his head, and raised his scimitar. But outside, the noise of the crowds got louder and louder; there was banging and clattering as some people began to scale the city walls. Why, they were breaking into the palace to save their beloved Aladdin! The vizier ran to a window and saw the multitude below yelling, 'Save Aladdin! Save Aladdin!'

'Sire,' said the vizier, 'I recommend that we stay the execution so as not to further rouse the fury of your people. The safety of your kingdom is at stake.'

'Halt!' The Emperor waved at the executioner, who lowered his scimitar.

'What have I done to deserve this?' Aladdin begged to know. 'What's happened?'

'I'll show you what's happened, you false wretch,' cried the Emperor, and dragged him to a window. 'Where is your palace? Where is my daughter? Use your cursed magic. Find her!'

Aladdin stared in horror, too stunned to speak. 'I … I … ' he stuttered.

'Bring me my daughter immediately, or lose your head.'

'Sire! Forty days. Give me forty days to find her,

and if I fail, you shall kill me,' begged Aladdin.

'Forty days it is! Now get out.'

Aladdin was flung out of the palace.

For three days, he wandered about like a madman, too distraught to know where he could start his search. People laughed at him when he asked, 'Has anyone seen my palace? Does anyone know where my wife is?' And all those who had once declared themselves to be his friend, turned their backs on him.

Finally, in despair, he wandered down to the riverbank intending to throw himself in. Clasping his hands together in prayer, he inadvertently rubbed the magic ring on his finger. The ring! How could he have forgotten the magic ring?

Immediately, a great genie rose above him, higher and higher, sending

Aladdin toppling backwards onto the bank. 'I am the genie of the ring. Speak, Master, and tell me what you desire.'

'Save my life,' pleaded Aladdin. 'Bring back my palace and my princess.'

'I am but the genie of the ring,' replied the genie. 'Only the far greater power possessed by the genie of the lamp can return your palace and the princess. But I can take you to her.'

'Take me then. Now, quickly, as soon as … '

But he had barely finished his demands when he found he had been transported to Africa, and dropped at the palace just under the window of the princess's bedchamber.

With a smile of exhaustion and delight, Aladdin fell into a deep sleep.

When he awoke the next morning,

it was to the sound of a window being opened near his head, and who should look out, but his own dear princess. When she saw him, she was overjoyed, and hurried away to open a side door to let him in.

They embraced and laughed and cried, and the princess told him that the wicked magician wanted her to forget her husband, and marry him – but she would rather die. And she wept again.

Aladdin said, 'Tell me, my beloved, what became of the lamp which stood on a shelf in the alcove?'

'Alas,' wept the princess. 'It's all my fault. I exchanged it for a new one from the magician. I didn't know ... '

'Where is it now?'

'The magician carries it with him everywhere, hidden beneath his robes,' answered the princess.

'Then I must get it back,' muttered Aladdin. 'I'll go now and think up a plan, but be sure to let me in by your own private door when I return.'

Once more out in the street, Aladdin had an idea. He stopped a poor man passing by, and offered to exchange clothes with him. The man was delighted, and soon Aladdin hurried away in his new disguise in search of a local apothecary. He gave the apothecary the name of a certain powder which he asked to buy, and handed over a number of gold coins. Then he quickly returned to the palace, and entered by the private door to his waiting princess.

'Dearest, I have here a special powder. Now listen carefully. Go and bathe in scented water, and dress in your most beautiful clothes. When the sorcerer comes to your apartment, greet him with your most gracious smile. After a while, suggest you have a drink together and then you must distract him so that you can pour this powder into his glass. Then your troubles will be over.'

The princess bravely agreed. She went away and bathed, then put on her finest robes, and decorated her hair with diamonds, knowing that only on her wedding day had she ever looked more lovely. That evening, the magician came to her door suggesting they sup together.

This time, he was pleased to see how graciously she received him. By the glimmering candlelight, she enchanted him with her chatter, and then suggested they drink to each other. The magician was delighted and hurried away to fetch a flagon of grape juice and two goblets. He poured out the juice, and turned briefly to set the flagon on a table. At that moment, the princess tipped the powder into his goblet, and held it up to him as he returned. She raised hers to her lips and smiled.

'Your health!' he exclaimed. He tipped back his goblet, swallowed his juice in one gulp, and fell back dead.

The princess opened the door and signalled Aladdin to come. 'We're free of this evil,' she cried, flinging her arms around him. 'Now can we go home?'

'Go to your chamber, dearest,' said Aladdin, 'and wait there while I complete what has to be done.' When she had gone, Aladdin hastily removed the lamp from the dead magician and rubbed it. Immediately the genie of the lamp came rushing out like a whirlwind, filling the room with his dark presence.

'I am the genie of the lamp. Your every wish is my command. Speak, Master, and I will obey.'

'Take me, the princess, this palace and everything in it back to Cathay from where it came.'

Sitting in her chamber, the princess only felt two tiny shocks: one when the palace lifted from the ground in Africa, and a moment later, when it was set down in Cathay. Meanwhile, her father, the Emperor, had awoken and, as usual, looked out of his window to mourn the loss of his daughter and to gaze sorrowfully at the empty space that was all that remained. But – what was this? When he looked out, the palace was back!

With what joy did the Emperor embrace his daughter, clasp Aladdin with relief, and order a ten-day feast to celebrate the happy ending.

Now Aladdin and his princess could live the rest of their lives in peace and happiness, couldn't they?

But no; the evil magician had a younger brother who, if anything, was even more wicked. When he heard of the death of his older brother, he cursed mightily and swore to take revenge. He made his way speedily to Cathay …

Scheherazade stopped abruptly, her eyes fixed on the eastern night sky, seeing the first grey glimmer of day.

'Don't stop, don't stop!' begged Shahriar. 'What happened? Tell me, I beg of you. I want to know what the younger brother did.'

Scheherazade shook her head sadly. 'Alas, Sire, my time has come to an end, and I fear I must die.'

'But the story hasn't ended. I don't know what happened. You can't just leave me hanging in the air.'

'It is your decree, Sire,' she said quietly, dropping her veil over her beautiful face.

'No, no! You must return – I must know how the story ends. Come back tonight, I command it.'

'Very well, Sire. Your every wish is my command.' And Scheherazade was led away.

And so every day, Dinasarde told her sister what happened next, and gave her a new story to continue, and every evening, Scheherazade returned to the King to complete the story and tell another one until a thousand and one nights of storytelling had passed. Finally she came to a stop. She had managed to save a thousand maidens from death, but could she save any more? Dinasarde could think of no more stories to tell her sister. As the next day was dawning, Scheherazade turned a pale face to the King. 'Well, it is almost sunrise, and I suppose I must die.'

'My dear Scheherazade,' replied the King tenderly. 'While you have been telling me stories, I have realized how noble and good you are, and that I was terribly mistaken to believe that all women were treacherous. I beg forgiveness to all those whose daughters I have wrongly killed, and I humbly ask if you will continue to be my wife?'

And so Scheherazade's plan worked. She and the King lived in peace, justice and harmony for many more thousands of nights, and it's very likely that Dinasarde found a few more stories up her sleeve, to pass on to her sister, for the King's enjoyment.